I0816452

THE MYTHOLOGY LIBRARY

Greek Myths

Don Nardo

San Diego, CA

Printed in the United States

For more information, contact:
ReferencePoint Press, Inc.
PO Box 27779
San Diego, CA 92198
www.ReferencePointPress.com

LIBRARY OF CONGRESS CATALOGING-IN-PUBLICATION DATA

Names: Nardo, Don, 1947- author
Title: Greek myths / by Don Nardo.
Description: San Diego, CA : ReferencePoint Press, Inc, 2026. | Series: The mythology library | Includes bibliographical references and index.
Identifiers: LCCN 2025024528 (print) | LCCN 2025024529 (ebook) | ISBN 9781678212346 library binding | ISBN 9781678212353 ebook
Subjects: LCSH: Mythology, Greek--Juvenile literature
Classification: LCC BL783 .N37 2026 (print) | LCC BL783 (ebook) | NLM 398.20938
LC record available at https://lccn.loc.gov/2025024528
LC ebook record available at https://lccn.loc.gov/2025024529

CONTENTS

THE OLYMPIAN GODS

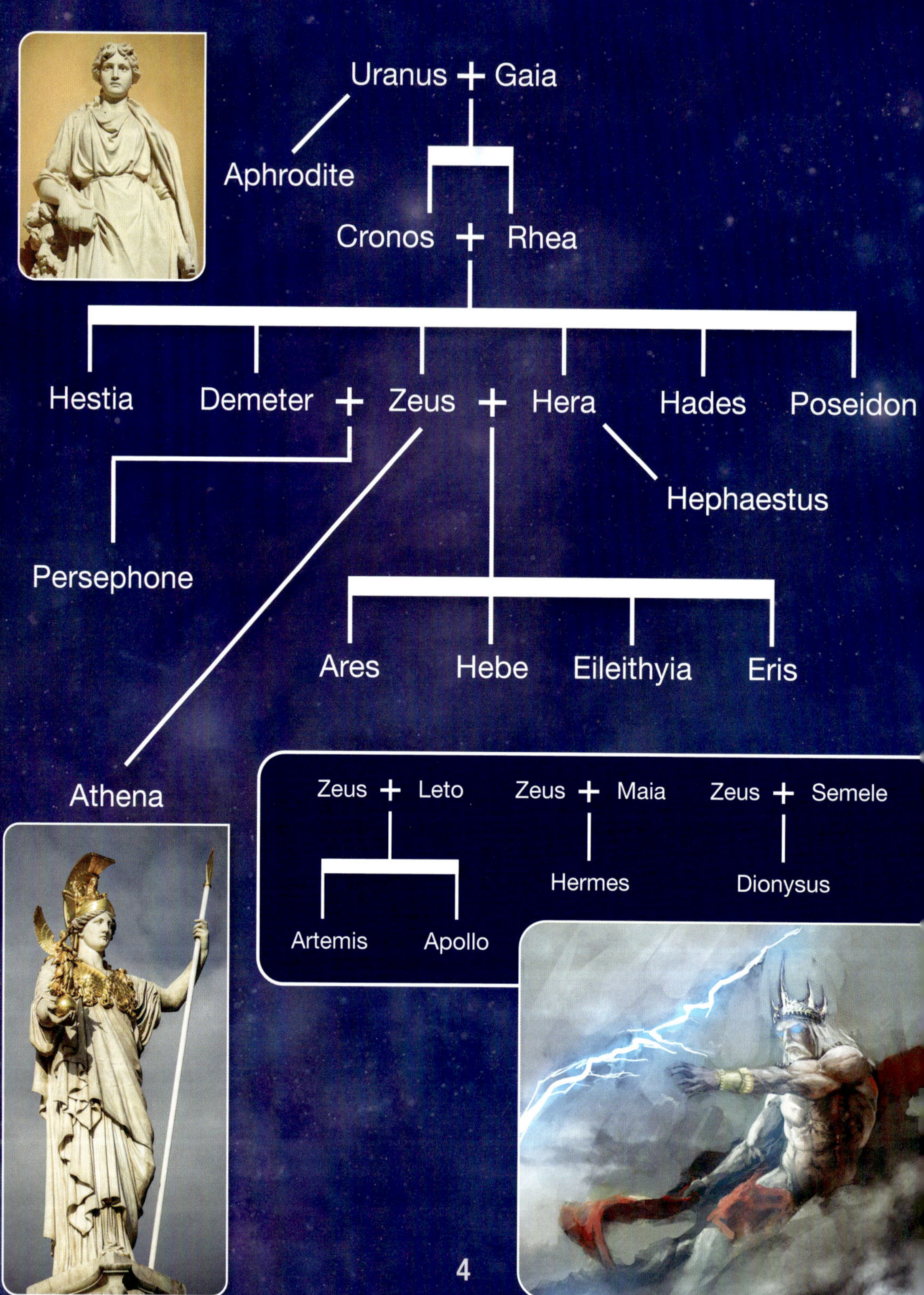

How the Greek Myths Came to Be

Thousands of years ago, in the Greek-speaking lands of the Mediterranean region, when children misbehaved parents might mention any number of bizarre creatures to scare their kids into correcting their behavior. To name only a few, they included dragons; a female monster so frightening that merely gazing at her turned someone to stone; and the Cyclopes, one-eyed giants who ate humans for lunch. Another scary creature feared by both children and adults in ancient Greece was Cerberus, the enormous three-headed dog said to guard the borders of the underworld. Legends claimed that the vicious beast would grab and eat any human soul trying to escape that death realm. Because Hades, god of the underworld, had placed the creature there expressly for that purpose, none of the heroes known for slaying monsters ever tried to kill it.

CERBERUS
The huge, three-headed hound that guarded the border of the underworld

However, that did not stop Eurystheus, king of the city of Tiryns (in southern Greece), from seeking to capture the hellhound and put it on display in his royal court. To carry out such a dangerous task, he sent for the greatest of all the ancient Greek heroes—the mighty Heracles (better known today as Hercules). On Eurystheus's order, the famous strongman traveled to the River Styx, which marked the boundary between the surface world and underworld. There, the strongman wrestled the creature into submission, tossed it into a cage, and transported it to Tiryns.

HERACLES
In later times called Hercules, the greatest of Greece's mythical heroic monster slayers

Thrilled with Heracles's daring feat, Eurystheus eagerly displayed the captured monster to his subjects. In time, however, the king increasingly feared that the beast might somehow escape. So he ordered Heracles to take Cerberus back to the dimly lit underworld, and the strongman did so without delay.

In ancient Greek eyes, of all the incredible deeds that Heracles performed, capturing and later releasing the fierce guardian of the land of the dead was seen as one of the greatest. In his play about the legendary hero, the Athenian dramatist Euripides sang his praises. The subduing of Cerberus, Euripides wrote, was "the crown of his journeys and glorious exploits."[1]

Lacking the Science of Archaeology

Every classical Greek learned the story of Heracles's capture of Cerberus, along with many dozens of other myths, when still very young. When used in a general manner, the term *classical Greeks* denotes the residents of the Greek-speaking lands from about 700 to 300 BCE. Spearheaded by the city-state of Athens, Greece's so-called golden age occurred during that period. Democracy, literature, architecture, philosophy, and science together blossomed as never before in human history. And over succeeding centuries these cultural achievements laid most of the foundations of Western (European-based) civilization.

To the Greeks of that bygone age, stories about Heracles and other daring heroes of the distant past were entertaining, but they were more than that. These stories were seen as integral parts of history. Most Greeks assumed that Heracles had been a real person and similarly that the famous Trojan War had actually happened. In that legendary conflict, the classical Greeks believed, an army of Greeks, including several warriors of heroic stature, had sacked the mercantile city of Troy (in Anatolia, now Turkey).

Heracles captures Cerberus, the three-headed guardian of the underworld.

The reality, however, was that the characters and events of those myths were not literally historical. Instead, they were composed of a mix of fabricated elements and mangled memories of people and events from earlier times. Because the Greeks lacked the science of archaeology, they had no idea how long ago those past peoples and events had existed. They also did not realize that Greece had been the site of a different civilization that had prospered and then vanished long before their own society had emerged. Modern historians call the period in which that earlier civilization thrived Greece's late Bronze Age (ca. 1600 to ca. 1150 BCE).

A Haphazard Myth-Making Process

Modern archaeologists have shown that the residents of Bronze Age Greece fell into two principal groups. On the big island of Crete and nearby islands dwelled the Minoans, who constructed several large structures that served as palaces, religious centers, and food-distribution hubs. The southern Greek mainland, meanwhile, was home to a people modern scholars call the Mycenaeans. They established a few small but powerful kingdoms, one centered in Athens.

For reasons that historians still debate, the prosperous Minoan–Mycenaean civilization fairly suddenly collapsed sometime between 1200 and 1100 BCE. The massive palaces were abandoned and fell into disrepair, while the arts and reading and writing skills all but disappeared. "In place of the palaces," archaeologists John Camp and Elizabeth Fisher write, "were tiny, unfortified settlements with a handful of small houses built with rubble walls and mud."[2]

As many aspects of civilized society vanished, Greece entered a three-century-long era that modern experts call its Dark Age (ca. 1100 to ca. 800 BCE). During those years, the people, largely poor and illiterate, lost contact with their own past. In the words of historian Thomas R. Martin, they "suffered from a virtual amnesia about the Bronze Age [civilization]." Some names and tales of prior events did survive, but in incomplete, disjointed ways. Roving minstrels called bards told and retold the stories about the past, embellishing and reshaping them. In this haphazard myth-making process, Martin explains, "storytelling, music, singing, and oral performances of poetry which surely had been part of Greek life for longer than we can trace, transmitted the most basic cultural ideas of the Greeks about themselves from generation to generation."[3]

Everyone's Precious Property

Thus, when the Dark Age ended in the early 700s BCE and a new Greek civilization steadily arose, its members possessed a large body of tales about a fabled past era. The emerging classical Greeks came to call it the Age of Heroes. This seemed appropriate because many of the more popular myths recounted the deeds of bigger-than-life heroes. In this way, great legendary warriors and monster slayers—among them Heracles, Achilles, Odysseus, and Jason—became familiar to nearly all Greeks.

At first, bards continued to keep the old stories alive orally. The most famous among them was the eighth-century-BCE poet Homer. Eventually, however, as the Greeks developed a workable writing system, they wrote the myths down. The epic poet Hesiod; playwrights Aeschylus, Sophocles, and Euripides; biographer Plutarch; and others ensured that those colorful tales would be preserved. And thereby, in the fullness of time, the classical Greeks' "vision of a heroic world," as the late scholar C.M. Bowra phrased it, reached modern society. The myths the Greeks cherished "as one of their most precious possessions"[4] became the prized property of people everywhere.

CHAPTER ONE

Creation of the World, Gods, and Humans

At first, all that existed was an incredibly disordered muddle of unconnected elements that swirled around and around in utter silence and without the tiniest glimmer of light. "In the whole universe there was nothing else," the late, great modern mythologist Edith Hamilton wrote. "All was black, empty, silent, endless." She added that that massive, spinning jumble was called "Chaos, the vast immeasurable abyss, outrageous as a sea, dark, wasteful, wild."[5]

Then, quite suddenly, out of total disorder sprang a small ounce of order. As some of the nonliving materials floating randomly within Chaos merged in just the right mixture, two slightly self-aware beings sprang into existence. Immense, and still formless, they were called Night and Erebus. At first, they were content to keep whirling and twirling through the darkness for more uncounted eons.

Finally, for reasons even the later gods could not explain, Night and Erebus embraced. From their union an egg-like mass formed. Over time it grew in size and complexity until it abruptly burst open, and out came an incomparably beautiful being. Called Eros, he was the very embodiment of pure love. Moreover, he possessed an innate longing to expel Chaos and replace it with logical, meaningful order. Thus, said Hamilton, "from darkness and from death, love was born, and with its birth, order and beauty began to banish blind confusion."[6]

Rapidly, guided by Eros's powerful will, the universe, which the Greeks would later come to call the cosmos, took coherent, useful form. The heavier elements settled out and became

EROS
The personification of love and light, said to have emerged from an egg in the midst of primeval Chaos

the earth, while the lighter materials floated upward and became the sky. Next, the creative Eros generated a huge burst of light, making the earth and the heavens visible for the first time. And mere minutes later, he produced a torrent of water that became the earth's oceans, lakes, and rivers.

Suddenly, a gigantic, intelligent spirit awakened. Gaia was that spirit's name. And when she gazed upward, she saw that another huge divinity was forming—Uranus, the embodiment of the sky. The two wasted no time in mating, which generated a flurry of offspring, all horribly misshapen. Among them, the early Greek poet Hesiod said, were the "unspeakable Kottos and Gyes and Briareus, insolent children, each with a hundred [hands], darting about, untouchable, and each had fifty heads standing upon his shoulders. . . . And these most awful sons of Mother Earth and Father Heaven were hated by their father from the first."[7]

Gaia and Uranus also gave birth to a brood of Cyclopes, the first of multiple races of those one-eyed giants. Uranus disliked them nearly as much as he did the Hundred-Handers he had sired. Would he and Gaia produce nothing but monsters?, he wondered with no small amount of concern.

The Universe Created the Gods?

The classical Greeks did not share Uranus's worry. They were aware that he and his mate, Gaia, would go on to create the first true race of gods—the Titans. The emergence of those deities would become the next chapter in the Greek saga of creation. The first chapter, encompassing the appearance of the earth and sky from Chaos, was essential to the Greek sense of purpose in nature. Like other ancient peoples, they longed to know where the world came from. And the first chapter of the creation story answered that question.

Yet the world's origins and other aspects of creation were not simply a matter of idle curiosity to the Greeks. They suspected that underlying nature were invisible, rational forces, and that it was inevitable that those forces would sooner or later force Chaos to become ordered and well organized. That idea—that nature itself was somehow inherently ordered and logical—was completely new to the world.

Moreover, early Greek thinkers took that then-unusual notion a crucial step further. Unlike most other ancient peoples, they speculated that the universe created the gods, rather than the other way around. That is, instead of one or more divine beings miraculously appearing or already existing and deciding to create the world, lifeless natural forces gave rise to self-aware beings, including divine ones.

Even though no one knew it at the time, this marked the birth of scientific thinking. And in the sixth century BCE, several Greek philosophers became, for all intents and purposes, the world's first scientists. Belief that the gods and their exploits in the myths

Night whirled through the darkness of Chaos until meeting Erebus.

were real remained widespread. But increasingly, people accepted that those beings were part of an existing natural order. "It was assumed, for the first time in history," the late popular scholar Rex Warner pointed out, that the universe is "an orderly system governed by laws which could be discovered by logical thought."[8]

Rhea, Cronos, and the Other Titans

Thus, while the Greeks came to accept that the gods were part of nature rather than its creators, people continued to perpetuate the age-old myths and delighted in telling and retelling them. That included other parts of the creation story, in which Gaia and Uranus finally managed to produce physically beautiful offspring. These Titans, as the Greeks called them, had human form, although they were much bigger and more powerful than the humans who would be created later.

RHEA
Wife of the leader of the Titans, Cronos, she gave birth to Zeus, Hera, and several of the other future Olympian deities

Some of the Titans were also admirable characters. Prometheus, for example, was known for his wisdom, fairness, and decency. Rhea was widely viewed as a good and caring mother. And some other Titans, like the sun god Hyperion and moon goddess Thea, performed their duties well.

In contrast, the leader of this earliest race of gods, Cronos, though physically imposing, was a dim-witted, mean-spirited bully. He forced his sister Rhea, against her will, to marry and mate with him. No less heinous was the way he treated their children. Paranoid as well as stupid, Cronos came to fear that those offspring might one day turn on him and threaten his rule. To prevent such a scenario, after the first child, Hera, was born, the chief Titan grabbed her and swallowed her in a single gulp. (The baby did not die because, being divine like her parents, she was immortal. So she remained very much alive deep within her father's huge body.) Cronos went on in similar fashion to swallow the next four infants Rhea birthed—Poseidon, Demeter, Hestia, and Hades.

Cronos, Uranus, and the Giants

Modern mythologists point out that the reason Cronos feared his children would eventually turn on him was that his own father, Uranus, had harbored the same fear about him. Indeed, Uranus had detested his own offspring, including Cronos, and treated them horribly. Meanwhile, Cronos's mother, Gaia, the Earth Mother, had become angry over that mistreatment. And hoping to punish her husband, she had urged Cronos to attack and if necessary kill Uranus. Armed with a razor-sharp sickle, Cronos ambushed his father and with a swing of the weapon sliced off the older god's genitals. That sent an immense spray of blood droplets flying through the air, and each droplet swiftly morphed into a barbaric giant. The Greek myth teller whom modern scholars call Pseudo-Apollodorus described these creatures as "unsurpassed in the size of their bodies and unconquerable by virtue of their power. They were frightening in appearance, with long hair that swept down from their heads and chins, and serpent-scales covering their lower limbs." These monsters later attacked the Olympian gods in a conflict the Greeks called the Gigantomachy (meaning "War of the Giants"), a battle the gods won.

Quoted in Theoi Greek Mythology, "Gigantes." www.theoi.com.

Disgusted by this barbaric behavior, Rhea was determined to stop it. To that end, when the sixth baby—Zeus—arrived, she concealed him, placed a big rock in a blanket, and handed it to her husband. Unaware of Rhea's trick, Cronos swallowed the rock and blanket whole and went about his business. Greatly relieved, Rhea carried baby Zeus to a cave on the island of Crete and asked two kindhearted nature deities to raise him there in secret.

A Tremendous Conflict

When Zeus was old enough, his mother informed him about the sad plight of his brothers and sisters. Horrified, he quickly devised a plan to free them. It included slipping a drug into Cronos's food that would make him vomit profusely, which he did. And one by one, out popped Hades, Hestia, Demeter, Poseidon, and Hera, all now grown into adults. These young gods were elated both to be free at last and to meet their sibling and savior, Zeus.

PROMETHEUS
The wisest of the Titans, who fought on Zeus's side in the Titanomachy and later created humans from clay

Meanwhile, Cronos, furious over being tricked, thought only about revenge. Determined to slay his six offspring, he started gathering some of the other Titans into a small but powerful army. Hearing of this, Zeus and his siblings concluded that they had no choice but to prepare for battle. Luckily for them, Prometheus and a few other Titans who detested Cronos joined their cause. Soon an enormous conflict erupted in which the two groups of deities clashed to decide who would control the cosmos. The classical Greeks called it the Titanomachy, meaning "War of the Titans."

The tremendous battle lasted for several years and did terrible damage to the earth. In his *Theogony*, Hesiod told how the ground cracked and swayed and the seas splashed violently back and forth. "High Mt. Olympus reeled from its foundation under

Rhea protected Zeus by handing Cronos a rock wrapped in a blanket instead.

the charge of the undying gods," he wrote. "They launched their grievous shafts [arrows and spears] upon one another, and the cry of both armies as they shouted reached to starry heaven."[9]

The Olympians Assume Power

Eventually, Zeus's side won the war. He ordered that Cronos and his followers be exiled to Tartarus, a dimly lit, desolate portion of the underworld. To ensure the prisoners would never escape, Zeus hired as their guards the fearsome Hundred-Handers earlier begotten by Gaia and Uranus.

The next few years witnessed the victors' efforts to clean up and restructure the earth's devastated surface. At the same time, they erected several magnificent palaces atop Greece's tallest peak, Mount Olympus. Thus, they became known as the Olympian gods. In their new world order, each of them became guardian of some aspect of nature or society. Zeus retained his leadership position, becoming the chief god. He asked Hera to be queen of the gods, as well as protector of marriage and women. Meanwhile, Demeter agreed to oversee agriculture; Hestia protected the family hearth; Poseidon took control of the seas; and Hades ruled the underworld. Another divinity, the beautiful Aphrodite, who had been born before the great war, became goddess of love.

As time went on, Zeus sired various children who also became Olympians. In Hesiod's words, "Zeus himself produced, from his own head, grey-eyed Athena,"[10] goddess of war and wisdom. And the chief god's son Ares became the male war god. Some other well-known Olympian deities were Apollo, god of prophecy; his sister Artemis, goddess of hunting and the moon; and the swift-footed Hermes, the messenger deity.

To Create a Race of Worshippers

The final chapter in the Greek creation tale came when the gods addressed the issue of animals, none of which yet existed. The deities wanted to fill every niche of nature with living creatures.

Moreover, at least some of those lesser beings should adore and serve the gods. Indeed, the Olympians reasoned, as divine, immortal beings, they deserved to have loyal worshippers.

To take on the task of crafting the animals and worshippers, Zeus turned to his leading adviser, the wise Prometheus, who happily accepted the job. According to the late historian and myth teller W.H.D. Rouse, the substance the Titan employed for fashioning those new living beings was moist clay. Initially, he "made this clay into all sorts of odd shapes." Some became horses, cows, pigs, fish, and snakes. Later, when he was ready to make the worshippers, he decided to make them god-shaped, standing upright with a head, two arms, and two legs. "In so doing," Rouse continued, "he made the first humans." Prometheus quickly became fascinated by and protective of these little beings. "He used to watch them hunting for food, and living in caves and holes, like ants or badgers. He determined to educate them as well as he could, and he was always their friend."[11]

A Tribute to Prometheus's Bravery

To the classical Greeks the Titan Prometheus was a gallant, inspiring character. He was humanity's creator and the one who gave humans the knowledge of fire. In the myth in which Zeus unjustly punished Prometheus by chaining him to a rock, the Greeks viewed the Titan as the hero and Zeus as the villain. This can be plainly seen in the various writings the Greeks produced about that myth. Arguably the most impressive and moving surviving example from those writings is the fifth-century-BCE Athenian playwright Aeschylus's superb play *Prometheus Bound*. That work is, overall, a tribute to the Titan's bravery and desire to help the humans he had created. The following lines, sympathizing with Prometheus's plight, are spoken by the members of the chorus. (In ancient Greek drama, the chorus was a group of supposedly unbiased characters who stood onstage and intermittently commented on the story as it unfolded.) At one point the chorus addresses the bound and tormented Prometheus, saying, "Only a heart of iron, a temper carved from rock, Prometheus, could refuse compassion for your pains. Had I known, I could have wished never to see this sight. Now that I have seen it, sorrow and anger wrack my heart."

Aeschylus, *Prometheus Bound*, in *Aeschylus: Prometheus Bound, The Suppliants, Seven Against Thebes, The Persians*, trans. Philip Vellacott. Penguin, 1961, p. 28.

As time went on, Prometheus's concern for his human creations increased. Because they had no concept of fire, they had to eat raw meat and they shivered in misery during the cold winters. Finally, the Titan could stand it no longer. Even though Zeus had expressly forbidden anyone to give the humans knowledge of fire, Prometheus did so. As a result, they were able to cook their food, warm themselves, and smelt metals to make tools and weapons and build a civilization.

It did not take long for Zeus to find out what had happened. And he was enraged. At his order, Prometheus was chained to a

Prometheus gave fire to humans, but as punishment he was chained to a boulder and every day an eagle tore out his liver.

boulder on a distant mountain peak. There, each day a large eagle tore out the deity's liver. That night the organ grew back, and the next morning the creature returned and repeated the brutal act.

Thus, the great cycle of creation that had begun with radiant Eros's emergence from Chaos ended with Prometheus's sacrifice for his beloved humans. The classical Greeks saw Prometheus as a hero of epic proportions and his defiance of Zeus as the pivotal moment of the entire creation narrative. They also believed that the Titan had done much more than make civilization possible for humans. In their view, by example, he showed them free will, courage, and righteous behavior. As Edith Hamilton put it, eventually the muscular hero Heracles "slew the eagle and released Prometheus from his bonds, and Zeus was willing to have this done. But why Zeus changed his mind . . . we do not know. One thing, however, is certain: in whatever way the two were reconciled, it was not Prometheus who yielded. His name has stood through all the centuries, from Greek days to our own, as that of the great rebel against injustice and the authority of power."[12]

CHAPTER TWO

Clash of Champions: The Trojan War

Ancient legends claimed that the cause of the famous Trojan War, in which thousands of Trojans and Greeks lost their lives, was the abduction of a Greek queen, Helen, by a Trojan prince, Paris. This made it sound like the war was mainly Paris's fault, and some classical Greeks did blame him. However, many others suggested that the fault lay more with a group of vain, selfish gods who swayed the young prince's actions. They pointed to the well-known myth routinely called "The Judgment of Paris."

That tale begins with young Paris quietly tending some sheep on a picturesque mountainside near his home city. What he did not know at that moment was that he was being watched by none other than the leader of the gods, mighty Zeus. A short while before, the lord of Olympus had been approached by his divine wife, Hera, and two other prominent female deities—Athena, goddess of war, and the love goddess Aphrodite. The three women had been heatedly arguing over which one was the most beautiful. And they now demanded that Zeus referee a contest that would decide the issue.

Zeus was wise enough to know that there was no upside to his judging such a contest among these hugely conceited women. No matter which goddess he chose, the other two were bound to be angry. It made much more sense, therefore, to find someone else to judge the competition. It was then that he remembered hearing that the Trojan Prince Paris had often bragged about being a first-rate judge of beauty. Looking down

APHRODITE
The goddess of love, who caused Sparta's queen, Helen, to fall in love with Prince Paris of Troy

from lofty Olympus's summit, Zeus spied young Paris on the hillside near Troy and resolved to get the contest over with as quickly as possible.

To that end, the four Olympians leaped into the air and in only a few minutes covered the more than 200 miles (322 km) separating northern Greece from Troy. Appearing before the startled Paris, the deities informed him that they wanted him to choose the most beautiful of the three goddesses. Seeing the offer as a great honor, he agreed.

In the minutes that followed, each of the women, in turn, attempted to bribe Paris into selecting her. Hera promised to crown him king of both Europe and Asia. Athena offered to make him a major hero of the impending Trojan–Greek conflict. Aphrodite claimed she would cause the most beautiful woman in the world to fall in love with him.

For Paris, the choice was clear. The promise of love and romance appealed to him more than all of the other offers. So, he picked Aphrodite as the winner of the contest. True to her word, that goddess cast a love spell on the ravishing Helen, queen of the Greek kingdom of Sparta. And when Paris soon traveled there on a diplomatic mission, Helen privately told him she was madly in love with him. Passionately, he returned those feelings. As a result, betraying her marriage to Sparta's king, Menelaus, she agreed to run away with Paris to Troy.

The Most Popular Mythical Narrative

Every child growing up in classical Greece heard this story. By the time they were teenagers, they could recite the story of Paris's judgment of the divine beauty contest in some detail. Moreover, every ancient Greek knew the details of all the myths that together told the story of the Trojan War. This was partly because that story was the most renowned and popular narrative in the entire canon of Greek myths.

Paris picks Aphrodite as the winner of the beauty contest, offering her an apple.

As for the source of that narrative, key elements of it appeared in *The Iliad*, one of the two great epic poems by the eighth-century-BCE bard Homer. To the Greeks, he was not merely a storyteller; rather, in their eyes he towered over all other myth tellers. His epics were not seen merely as entertaining literature, which they were, but also as pivotal historical, social, political, and ethical guidelines. In the words of the late, prolific historian Michael Grant, Homer's works were the Greeks' "greatest civilizing influence." As such, those epics gained "universal esteem and reverence as sources of general and practical wisdom, as arguments for heroic yet human nobility and dignity, as incentives to vigorous [and] manly action, and as mines of endless quotations and commentaries, the common property of Greeks everywhere."[13]

The Iliad, which describes the Trojan conflict during its tenth and final year, was not written all at once. Modern experts think that shorter and more elementary versions of it appeared sometime in the tenth or ninth century BCE, during the Dark Age preceding the rise of the classical Greeks. Initially, the collection of myths that would become Homer's masterpiece passed from one generation to another orally. Traveling storytellers publicly recited them from memory, and each added a few new details and improved existing lines and phrases. In this way, the work grew longer and more polished over time.

Eventually, the Trojan War narrative reached Homer, the last and apparently most talented bard to shape it. His version was the one the classical Greeks finally wrote down at some point in the 600s BCE. Committing the story to parchment froze and preserved it in the superb form that every subsequent generation has inherited and adored.

The Quarrel Between Kings

Throughout those generations, one of the most popular subplots of the Trojan War myth has been the love affair between Paris and Helen. Numerous poems, plays, and movies have focused on it. Yet although those lovers are key players in the story, they are not the protagonists, or leading characters. That distinction falls to the war's primary warrior-heroes, including some of the Greek kings who prosecuted the long siege of Troy. One was Agamemnon, king of Mycenae and brother of Sparta's King Menelaus, who called on the other Greek monarchs to help him get his wife back. Another warrior-king was Odysseus, of the island kingdom of Ithaca (and the lead character in Homer's other epic, *The Odyssey*).

ACHILLES
The leading character in the Trojan War myth and the greatest of the Greek warrior-heroes who fought at Troy

The main protagonist of the Trojan War myth, however, is Achilles. Ruler of Phthia, in central Greece, he was the most fearsome of all the Greeks who fought at Troy. And much of the military action of the war's later stages revolved around him and his strong influence over his fellow Greeks. At first, he led his countrymen in winning several battles fought before Troy's towering walls. Yet the Trojans, often led by Paris's brother, Prince Hector, also had many victories. So the conflict became a stalemate.

That situation changed, however, when Achilles and Agamemnon argued loudly over ownership of an attractive slave woman. After Agamemnon took her for himself, Achilles angrily refused to leave his tent. He and his soldiers, he announced, would neither fight nor lead the Greeks in battle unless Agamemnon relented.

This put the Greeks at a major disadvantage, and soon they began losing battles as Hector led the Trojans in one victory after another. In the most dramatic of these skirmishes, that leading Trojan warrior led a furious attack on the Greek camp. "His

The Homeric Question

One of the Greek storytellers who publicly recited literary works, Homer was said to have created the final versions of two already existing epic poems. One, *The Iliad*, describes the events of the last year of the renowned Trojan War. The other work, *The Odyssey*, tells about the later exploits of Odysseus, one of the Greek kings who took part in the conflict. Homer's exact birth year is unknown. And in fact, too little is known about him to absolutely confirm that he was a real person. Based on later writings by Greek historians, along with the literary evidence of the epics themselves, however, modern scholars are confident that he did exist. They estimate that he lived sometime in the 700s BCE.

Another mystery surrounding Homer is whether or not he actually contributed to both epics. Some experts have suggested that he might have expanded and finalized only one of them. But most scholars say that his unique use of vocabulary and literary style points makes it likely that he authored both works. Attempts to answer these and other questions about Homer continue—part of the debate known as the "Homeric question."

The slave girl, Briseis, is brought to Agamemnon after he and Achilles argued.

men came [charging] after him with a deafening roar," Homer wrote, "while the whole [Trojan] force behind them took up the [battle] cry."[14]

Achilles, Patroclus, and Hector

Some of the Greeks who were trying to defend the besieged camp rushed into Achilles's tent and begged him to come out and fight. But he still refused, citing Agamemnon's own refusal to give back the slave girl. Witnessing this exchange, Achilles's best friend, Patroclus, had an idea. If Achilles himself would not fight, perhaps that great champion's armor might in a sense fight in his stead. Removing his own armor, Patroclus daringly donned Achilles's splendid golden battle array, ran outside, and threw himself into the fight.

When the closest Trojans recognized Achilles's distinctive armor, they naturally thought that Achilles himself had reentered the fray. And many Trojans were suddenly afraid and began retreating toward the city. The overconfident Patroclus gave chase and soon fought one-on-one with several Trojans. During these encounters, some of those warriors managed to dent the golden armor and to wound its wearer. One Trojan even knocked the golden helmet to the ground, revealing that it was not Achilles but Patroclus who had been wearing it.

Mere seconds later, valiant Hector appeared. Seeing that Patroclus was, in Homer's words, "creeping wounded from the field," Hector "struck him with a spear in the lower part of the belly, driving the bronze clean through. Patroclus fell with a thud, and the whole Greek army was appalled."[15] To the mortally wounded Patroclus, Hector said, "You thought you would sack my town [and] make Trojan women slaves. . . . You were a fool [and] now the vultures here are going to eat you up."[16]

Not long after the brave but impulsive Patroclus breathed his last, Achilles learned about what had transpired. A changed man, the golden armor's true owner instantly rejoined the Greek army and led an attack that rapidly drove the Trojan troops back inside the city. Only a single Trojan fighter, bold Hector, did not retreat. He purposely stayed outside the walls, waiting for Achilles to meet him in single combat.

PATROCLUS
Achilles's best friend, who donned Achilles's armor and entered battle, with tragic consequences

Troy's leading warrior did not have to wait long. The Greeks formed ranks outside the city's front gate, preparing to watch the two champions come to death grips. Meanwhile, Trojans of all ages watched from the ramparts above. With trepidation, they saw Achilles stride outward from the Greeks' bronze-clad ranks and face off with his adversary.

There was a long pause as the two fighters eyed each other with disdain. Then abruptly, Homer said, "Hector charged, brandishing his sharp sword [and] Achilles sprang to meet him, inflamed with savage passion." Seconds later, the two men crashed together with a loud clanging of metal on metal, as loud cheers rang out from the observers on both sides. The fight that followed was gripping and pitiless. For a while it appeared to be evenly matched. But in time Achilles saw an opening and shoved his spear forward into his enemy's neck. "Hector came down in the dust, and the great Achilles triumphed over him," Homer wrote. The inevitable onset of death "cut Hector short and his disembodied soul took wing for the House of Hades [the underworld]."[17]

After what appeared to be an evenly matched fight, Achilles found an opening and thrust his sword into Hector's neck.

Achilles's Attempt to Avoid the War

Among the many minor myths that make up the larger Trojan War narrative is one that describes the great Greek warrior Achilles's initial attempts to avoid going to Troy. One day, the story goes, he received a message from Menelaus, king of Sparta. The Spartan ruler told him how Troy's Prince Paris had abducted Sparta's queen, Helen. Menelaus asked Achilles to join a Greek effort to retrieve her. Achilles's first impulse was to join the expedition. But when he mentioned the matter to his mother, the sea goddess Thetis, she frowned and told him not to do it. She explained that many years before she had heard a divine prophecy say that if the Greeks and Trojans ever clashed, her son would die in the conflict. Hoping to keep Achilles safe, Thetis secretly took him to the house of the young man's wealthy uncle. There, Achilles wore women's clothes day and night to make sure no one recognized him. Meanwhile, Menelaus sent Odysseus, king of Ithaca, who was known for his cleverness, to track down Achilles. Odysseus eventually found him at the uncle's house, saw through the female disguise, and convinced him to join the expedition to Troy.

Down the Corridors of Time

That memorable moment of success for the Greeks and their powerful champion was fleeting. The gloating Achilles tied Hector's legs to the back of a chariot and dragged the body around Troy's walls several times as the Trojans grimly watched. Fuming with rage, Paris, who was a skilled archer, finally seized his bow and sent an arrow sailing downward. With amazing precision, the shaft pierced the one part of Achilles's body—his heel—that was vulnerable to injury. The strike caused him to topple from the moving vehicle. Seconds later, his soul began to follow Hector's toward Hades's dark realm.

The war continued. But both sides were weary of the long decade of almost relentless fighting. At that point, crafty Odysseus devised a plan to achieve a quick victory. According to Edith Hamilton, he ordered some skilled carpenters to "make a huge wooden horse, which was hollow and so big that it could hold a number of men." Odysseus himself led the small group of commandos who climbed inside. Leaving the lofty object in the plain before Troy, the rest of the Greeks boarded their ships and sailed away. To the Trojans, Hamilton continued, "only one conclusion seemed possible. The Greeks had given up."[18] Accordingly, the jubilant Trojans dragged the horse into the city and celebrated all day and into the night.

But the truth was that the Greeks had not given up. Later, as the Trojans slept, Odysseus and his men stealthily exited the horse. They opened the gates for the Greek army, which had sailed back under the cover of darkness. Troy was doomed. But thanks to Homer and the other Greek bards, the story of its brave defenders' efforts to repulse the attacking Greeks would echo down the corridors of time for countless centuries to come.

CHAPTER THREE

Perilous Voyages of Epic Adventure

Odysseus's plan to use a huge wooden horse to trick the Trojans into thinking the Greeks had quit the siege of Troy had worked. Troy fell, and like the other Greeks, Odysseus looked forward to returning to his homeland. But that would not happen for quite some time, thanks to the foolish acts of one Greek soldier. As the Greeks sacked the city, one of them unwisely desecrated a local shrine dedicated to the war goddess Athena. Outraged, she called on her brother, Poseidon, to help her punish all of the invading soldiers. Glad to help, the lord of the seas conjured up a massive storm that blew hundreds of the Greek ships off course. The ship captains managed to get most of the vessels back to Greece within two or three weeks.

The twelve ships that Odysseus had brought to Troy from Ithaca ten years before were not among them. Those twelve lost their bearings and began to wander from one unknown land to another. Along the way they experienced a potent mix of high adventure, increasing homesickness, and frightening danger.

Typical were the strange events that occurred when they landed on an uncharted island not long after the storm had abated. Its residents were known as the Lotus-Eaters because they ate only lotus plants that grew on the island. Several of the Greeks sampled those plants. Almost immediately, they became idle and sluggish and forgot all about their homeland. In Homer's story, Odysseus later recalls, "I had to use force to bring them back to the ships." Once on board, he chained those men to their oars to keep them from going back ashore. "I then commanded the rest of my loyal band to embark with all speed on their fast ships, for fear that others of them might eat the lotus and think no more of home."[19]

The Cave of the Cyclops

Not long after departing the land of the Lotus-Eaters, the wandering Greeks arrived at another uncharted island. Shortly after going ashore with a few men to gather food and water, Odysseus learned that the local residents were Cyclopes. This particular tribe of one-eyed giants, it turned out, were primitive, savage, and, in Odysseus's words, dwelled in mountain caves, "where each man is lawgiver to his children and his wives, and nobody cares a jot for his neighbors."[20]

POLYPHEMUS
The Cyclops who trapped Odysseus and several other Greeks in a cave

During the search for food, the Greek shore party found some sheep and goats in a cave. The cave's inhabitant, a giant Cyclops named Polyphemus, had gone out. Finding no one at home, the men hoped to grab some of the animals and head for the ships. But just as they were preparing to leave, Polyphemus returned. To keep them from escaping with his animals, the Cyclops placed an enormous boulder at the cave's entrance, trapping the Greeks inside.

As Homer tells it, Odysseus asked the Cyclops to follow the laws of hospitality and treat his men with respect. Polyphemus only laughed. "You must be a fool," he chortled. In the next instant, he seized two of the Greeks, pounded their heads against the cave floor, and proceeded to eat them raw, bones and all. "We could do nothing," Odysseus later said, "but weep and lift up our hands to Zeus in horror at the ghastly sight."[21]

The Cyclops killed several more Greeks before Odysseus and his last few men used a sharpened wooden stake to blind him and escape. But although they made it safely to the ships, they quickly learned of further dangers ahead. As the Greeks sailed

The cyclops Polyphemus brings firewood back to his cave, where Odysseus and his men are trapped.

away, they heard Polyphemus call out to his father, the sea god Poseidon, for help. The men were horrified. It was Poseidon who had caused them to become lost in the first place. And now that they had made a divine enemy, they fully expected to experience the god's wrath.

The Sole Survivor

Angering the sea god did indeed turn out to be catastrophic for Odysseus's party, but not right away. As they journeyed toward home, Odysseus and his men arrived at the floating island of Aeolus, god of the winds. When they asked Aeolus to help them get home, the wind god agreed to aid them. Toward that end, he placed a bag on the flagship and made them promise not to open the bag. Ithaca was actually in sight in the distance when some of the sailors foolishly opened the bag, prompting the angry wind god to blow the ships back across uncharted seas.

Not long afterward, the expedition reached the island of a people called the Laestrygonians. There, eleven of the twelve vessels docked. Odysseus, who had remained on the flagship, anchored at a distance, watched in horror as the island's inhabitants attacked the ships' crews. It turned out that the Laestrygonians were cannibals. The men on the eleven ships died horrible deaths, leaving Odysseus and his remaining crew no choice but to flee for their lives.

All the while, Poseidon had been biding his time, waiting for just the right moment to punish Odysseus and his men. And now he saw his chance. He blew the last ship toward a huge monster named Scylla, in whose jaws most of Odysseus's remaining men died. The rest perished in a nearby whirlpool called Charybdis. Eventually, Odysseus, the expedition's sole survivor, boarded a small raft, and Poseidon sent a massive storm to wreck it.

How Odysseus Outwitted the Cyclops

Odysseus was well known for being both clever and wise. He demonstrated both qualities to outwit the Cyclops Polyphemus. Having trapped the Greek foraging party in his cave, that savage creature demanded to know the name of the group's leader. Odysseus thought about it carefully before answering. "Nobody," he finally said. Later in the ordeal, after the monster had eaten several of the Greeks, they managed to sharpen a wooden pole and jam it into the Cyclops's single eye. Blinded as he was, he could not stop the escaping men. According to Homer, Polyphemus was in a frenzied state. He pulled out the pole, tossed it aside, and then "raised a great shout for the other Cyclopes who lived in neighboring caves along the windy heights. These [giants], hearing his screams, came up [and], gathering outside the cave, asked, 'What on earth is wrong with you Polyphemus? Why must you disturb the peaceful night?' [Polyphemus answered] 'O my friends, it's Nobody's treachery [that] is doing me to death!'" If nobody was hurting him, the other Cyclopes said, there was nothing they could or should do. So they went away.

Homer, *Odyssey*, trans. E.V. Rieu. Penguin, 1987, p. 150.

Just as it seemed all was lost, Athena took pity on Odysseus. On the one hand, she admired him, seeing his cleverness as mirroring her own plentiful wisdom. On the other, she decided that by this time he had suffered enough. So she intervened and saw to it that after twenty long years of sailing, he finally made it home to his wife Penelope. In Homer's words, "Glad indeed they were to lie once more together in the bed that had known them long ago."[22] In a final, generous gesture, Athena delayed the coming of the dawn to give the reunited lovers extra time to reconnect.

Heroes on Dangerous, Magical Journeys

The classical Greeks loved stories about epic quests in which heroic characters faced various monsters, natural disasters, and other dangers. And for Greeks of all ages, Odysseus's ten-year journey through a host of hazards was the ultimate expression of that kind of adventure tale. It is no wonder, therefore, that by his or her early teens, every Greek child could recite long passages of Homer's *Odyssey* by heart.

After sailing for twenty years, Odysseus finally returned home to his wife, Penelope.

Moreover, the Greeks were not the only people of past ages who related to and enjoyed such myths. According to the late, great modern mythologist Joseph Campbell, most ancient mythologies contain at least one such epic adventure. He called that kind of story "the hero's journey." Typically, he wrote, all of those tales feature a number of shared themes and plot points. As the quest begins, Campbell said, the hero leaves his home and "is lured, carried away, or else voluntarily proceeds, to the threshold of adventure." He then "journeys through a world of unfamiliar yet strangely intimate forces, some of which severely threaten him, some of which give magical aid." During the quest, Campbell continued, the hero undergoes one or more major, often dangerous ordeals, manages to survive them all, and finally, at journey's end, he "reemerges from the kingdom of dread"[23] and makes it to his home.

The Rightful Heir to the Throne

For the classical Greeks, whose collection of myths featured several heroic quests, the only one that came close to Odysseus's journey in scope and excitement was the voyage of the *Argo*. The expedition of the *Argo*, commanded by the hero Jason, was memorably described in the *Argonautica* (Voyage of the Argo). Widely popular across the ancient Mediterranean world, that nearly six-thousand-line epic poem was penned in the third century BCE by the Greek writer Apollonius of Rhodes.

As recounted in that work, Jason grew up in obscurity not knowing that he was the rightful heir to the throne of Iolcos, a small kingdom in central Greece. As a young man, however, he learned that his father, King Aeson, had been illegally deposed by the present ruler, Pelias. Boldly, Jason confronted the usurper and demanded that he step down in favor of the lawful king—Jason himself.

PELIAS
A villain who usurped the throne of the kingdom of Iolcos from Jason's father

The corrupt and dishonest Pelias pretended to agree with that claim and falsely promised he would indeed abdicate the throne. But first, Jason must carry out a special mission that would prove he was fit to rule. That mission was to find and bring back the legendary Golden Fleece. The skin of a magical ram, it was rumored to be somewhere in a faraway land called Colchis. Pelias secretly hoped that Jason would die on that long, dangerous trip—eliminating the threat to his power.

Saved by a Goddess

Meanwhile, Jason wasted no time beginning preparations for the voyage. For a vessel, he managed to get the exceptionally seaworthy *Argo*, named for its builder, Argus. And for his crew, who came to be called the Argonauts, Jason gathered together an impressive group of warriors, among their number the heroic strongman and monster slayer Heracles.

It did not take long for Jason to realize that he was fortunate to have such a capable crew, for the trip proved to be fraught with danger from the start. Not long after heading northward for the Black Sea, where Colchis was said to lie, the *Argo* approached

The Argonauts and the Harpies

As they navigated the Black Sea on their way to Colchis, the Argonauts stopped briefly in Anatolia (what is now Turkey) to gather food and water. There they came upon an aged man named Phineus. Terribly emaciated, he was clearly close to death from starvation. He proceeded to explain that after he had committed only a minor offense, the leader of the gods, Zeus, had punished him severely. Each time Phineus tried to eat a meal, out of nowhere came the Harpies, flying creatures with sharp claws and a sickening stench, who stole his food. Out of pity, Jason ordered his men to help old Phineus. As it happened, two of the Argonauts, Zetes and Calais, were the sons of a wind god and thereby were able to fly. So the next time the Harpies appeared, those two warriors chased them away and pursued them into the clouds. The men drew their swords and were about to slay the Harpies when Iris, goddess of rainbows, intervened. Sister to the creatures, she agreed to keep them away from Phineus if the Argonauts spared their lives. The deal was struck, and thereafter the old man ate all his meals in peace.

Medea and Jason take the fleece from the dragon while it is sleeping.

the much-dreaded Clashing Rocks. They consisted of two tall, sheer cliffs that rose on either side of a narrow channel that the travelers had no choice but to navigate. Those towering crags ceaselessly shook, causing boulders to rain down and create enormous waves that over time had destroyed many ships. As Apollonius described it, the rocks collided "face to face with a resounding crash . . . [and] the sea gave a terrific roar [as it] came surging in, and a great wave broke against the cliffs."[24]

While Jason was trying to determine how to get through the treacherous channel, quite unexpectedly the war goddess Athena, who greatly admired Jason, appeared. According to Apollonius, "Holding onto the hard rocks with her left hand, she pushed the ship through with the other. And the *Argo* clove the air like a winged arrow."[25]

Encounters with Strange, Scary Creatures

The Argonauts had other dangerous encounters on their way to Colchis. One included a confrontation with the Harpies, repulsive flying creatures with razor-sharp teeth and claws. Another consisted of bloody combat with a flock of deadly metal-beaked birds.

Moreover, such battles with strange, scary creatures continued even after the *Argo* reached the fabled land of Colchis. There, the local king, Aeetes, refused to give up the fleece unless Jason proved himself worthy. As a test of that worth, the lead Argonaut had to tame and yoke two fire-breathing bulls, use them to plow the soil and plant dragons' teeth, and then fight an army of warriors who swiftly sprang up from those seeds.

MEDEA
A princess of Colchis and a sorceress, she fell in love with Jason and helped him steal the Golden Fleece

Aeetes had purposely intended these feats to be impossible to perform. But Jason had help from an unlikely source. Medea, the king's daughter, was a sorceress. She used magic to aid Jason, with whom she had fallen in love at first sight. She also helped him seize the fleece, which hung in a tree guarded by a large dragon. After showing Jason the location of the tree, she used drugs to lull the creature into a drowsy state to keep it from attacking him.

When Aeetes heard the fleece was gone, he was furious but could do nothing about it. From a hilltop near the sea, he watched helplessly as the Argonauts, accompanied by Medea, sailed triumphantly for Greece. Thus did the voyage of the *Argo*, like Odysseus's wanderings, witness much strife and death along the way but end on a positive note.

Daring Heroes Who Slew Monsters

Back in an era now lost in the mists of time, a ship loaded with warriors clad in bronze armor neared the northern coast of the large Aegean island of Crete. The commander of those soldiers, the Athenian prince Theseus, reminded them to stay quiet as they went ashore. He hoped this would ensure a successful surprise attack.

The initial strategy was to overpower the palace guards at Knossos, capital of the Cretan realm ruled by King Minos. For years Minos had been kidnapping Athenian teenagers and bringing them back to Knossos. He had recently done this yet again, snatching fourteen Athenian teenagers—seven boys and seven girls. A move designed to intimidate the Athenians, Minos's overall goal was to keep Athens subservient to and dependent on Crete. As for the young hostages, they were doomed. It was said that Minos tossed them into the Labyrinth, a maze of tunnels beneath his palace. There they were killed and devoured by the Minotaur, a half-human, half-bull monster with a ravenous appetite.

A Risky Rescue Effort

For years Theseus's father, King Aegeus, had been unable to stop the seizure of the young Athenians. But Theseus finally convinced the older man that a surprise raid might work. At the very least, the prince argued, it might rescue the present batch of hostages before they met their untimely deaths in the Labyrinth. Theseus also stated his goal to kill the murderous Minotaur. It was indeed risky, both men agreed, but worth a try. As a precaution, according to the first-century-CE Greek writer

MINOTAUR
A half-man and half-bull creature; the Cretan King Minos kept it in a maze below his palace

Plutarch, "Aegeus gave the [ship's] pilot a second sail, a white one, and ordered him on the return voyage to hoist the white canvas if Theseus were safe, but otherwise to sail with the [standard] black sail as a sign of mourning."[26]

When the Athenian vessel landed near Minos's palace, Theseus and his soldiers rushed forward, slew the guards as planned, and gained temporary control of the building. Minos was nowhere to be found, but Theseus now had access to the Labyrinth's entrance. Carrying a torch and accompanied by two of his men, he swiftly descended into its dark corridors and soon found the hostages, who were still alive.

As the soldiers led the youths to safety, Theseus moved deeper into the maze. There, a few minutes later, he encountered the infamous Minotaur. The huge, repulsive beast seemed surprised

Theseus kills the Minotaur, a half-human, half-bull monster.

to see an adult human in its lair. Before it could gather its wits and attack, Theseus thrust the torch forward, blinding it. Stunned and screaming, it collapsed backward. Theseus then leaped onto it and used his sword to slice off its head and limbs.

Having rescued the hostages and slain the Minotaur, the Athenians sailed for home. As they approached Athens, they were still celebrating the successful mission; and as Plutarch wrote, both Theseus and his pilot forgot "to hoist the [white] sail which was to signal their safe return." Watching from atop a rocky hill, Aegeus "in despair threw himself down from the cliff and was killed."[27] Later, the legend claims, in the old king's memory the Athenians named the waterway bordering Greece's eastern coast the Aegean Sea.

A Handful of Special Heroes

Theseus and other noted monster slayers occupied a special place in the grand corpus, or collection, of myths inherited from the Age of Heroes. Warriors such as Achilles and Hector were memorable for their battle exploits, but the monster killers had an extra, exotic dimension. Only they had had the daring, skill, and at times divine connections to confront and vanquish creatures that were forces of nature in their own rights.

Stories about the monstrous natural forces found in the Age of Heroes provided the classical Greeks with a way to understand their own existence and their place in the world. They thought that during that long-ago time period the world was emerging from a state of chaos and barbarism. And the dragons, ogres, flying fiends, and other monsters mentioned in the myths were among the last remnants of the primitive past. Thus, by eradicating those beasts, the heroes helped make civilized life possible for human beings. Ridding the world of monsters, scholar and mythologist John Mancini writes, can therefore "be seen as a symbolic act of taming the wild." Those scary creatures threatened humanity's very survival and thereby "embodied all the natural forces the ancients would have feared. Slaying them meant slaying fear itself."[28]

Slayer of the Theban Dragon

Of the several legendary monster slayers the classical Greeks celebrated, Cadmus was one of the more memorable. Born in Phoenicia (now the coastal region of Israel), he was drawn into Greek affairs thanks to the actions of the chief Olympian god, Zeus. When Cadmus was in his late teens, his sister Europa was kidnapped by that powerful deity. And when Zeus took her to faraway Greece, the concerned Cadmus followed. The initial problem the young man faced was where to look for his sister. So he consulted the renowned oracle at Delphi (in central Greece), a priestess who answered questions posed by visitors. The oracle told Cadmus he should put aside looking for Europa; instead, he should establish a new city not far from Delphi. Accepting that advice, the young man proceeded to found one of Greece's premier cities, Thebes. Like the residents of all cities, the Thebans needed supplies of clean water. But the nearest mountain stream was guarded by an enormous dragon that devoured anyone who tried to drink from it. In a show of incredible courage, Cadmus drew his sword and attacked and killed the creature. Later generations of Greeks never forgot the fearless monster slayer who made a great city possible.

At first glance, one might assume that to overcome such intimidating natural forces those heroes must have possessed magical, or even godlike powers. Yet that was not the case. As W.H.D. Rouse pointed out, the monster slayers were very human and lived "in the world among mankind." Moreover, "they were not immortal. Their bodies died." Yet the people across the Mediterranean sphere whom they rescued from the monsters saw them as bigger and bolder than life and eminently more worthy than normal people. Furthermore, the gods generally agreed with that view. Therefore, says Rouse, those deities made sure that after Theseus and the other heroes like him died, their souls "lived still"[29] in the Islands of the Blessed—a paradise-like portion of the underworld.

The Mighty Heracles

When the classical Greeks told and retold the stories of the monster slayers of the Age of Heroes, it was generally agreed that they were all extraordinary individuals. Nevertheless, one of their number—Heracles—stood out above all the others. (The ancient Romans came to call him Hercules, the name he is best known by today.)

In addition to being fearless, big-hearted, and ethical in the extreme, Heracles was incredibly strong. In large part he had inherited his physical strength from his father Zeus, leader of the Olympian gods. Infamous for his various affairs with mortal women, Zeus had sired Heracles by sleeping with Alcmene, a princess of Mycenae (a small kingdom in southern Greece). That made Heracles semidivine. And though he sympathized with and often fought to protect humans, he took much pride in his heavenly ancestry and the powers that came with it. As Edith Hamilton put it, "he considered himself on an equality with the gods—and with some reason. Whenever he fought with anyone," she wrote, the outcome was certain from the start. "He could be overcome only by a supernatural force."[30]

That beings and forces spawned on earth could not defeat Heracles partly explains his success in killing, capturing, or chasing away numerous formidable, scary creatures. Among the earliest of the monsters he encountered was a large lion that was terrifying the inhabitants of the countryside near Thebes (in south-central Greece). Still in his teens but already fantastically muscular, Heracles tracked down the beast and wrestled it into submission, breaking many of its bones in the process.

EURYSTHEUS
A Greek king who challenged the hero Heracles to perform twelve incredibly difficult tasks—the so-called labors

The famous strongman slew a much larger lion when he was in his twenties. This was the first of a series of twelve so-called labors performed for the Greek king Eurystheus. Killing the so-called Nemean Lion made Heracles famous throughout the Mediterranean world of his day. People everywhere were enthralled by hearing the story of how he used his bare hands to strangle the giant cat. Later, also at Eurystheus's request, Heracles seized control of and eventually tamed a herd of huge, flesh-eating horses.

Heracles defeated many formidable monsters, including the dragon Ladon.

One of the most famous victories of the mighty Heracles, as he came to be known far and wide, was overcoming the so-called Stymphalian birds. These deadly creatures had beaks made of bronze. They had metallic feathers as well. Worse still, they loved to eat human flesh. They "shot at people with their steel-tipped feathers," wrote Michael Grant and fellow historian John Hazel. "Heracles got rid of them by means of a bronze rattle" created for him by the Olympian god of forges, Hephaestus. Using the rattle to confuse and frighten the vicious birds, the strongman, who was also a skilled archer, "shot many of them with his arrows."[31] Overcome with fear, the few surviving birds flew far away from the Greek lands, never to return.

On the Island of the Gorgons

Although the creatures that Heracles killed or captured are well known in Greek folklore, by far the most famous monster in all of Greek mythology is Medusa. Along with her sisters, Stheno and

Euryale, she was one of the three wicked and dangerous beings known as the Gorgons. They were said to have tusks protruding from their cheeks; long, slimy tongues hanging from their mouths; and hissing snakes for hair.

Ancient stories claimed Medusa had an added trait that made her the scariest of the unsightly sisters. It was the ability to petrify, or turn to stone, any animal or human who simply gazed on her. This made her a serious threat to humanity. A number of brave young warriors considered trying to eliminate that threat. The problem was that no one knew where she lived. Moreover, no one could think of a way to kill her without looking at her, which was instantly lethal.

Eventually, however, a young man named Perseus appeared on the scene. A son of Zeus and a mortal woman named Danae, he was very protective of his mother. So when a tyrant, Polydectes, king of the Aegean island of Seriphos, demanded that Danae marry him, Perseus objected. Fearing that if he simply killed Perseus it might kindle Zeus's wrath, Polydectes devised an alternate scheme to get rid of the young man. The king told Perseus that if he brought back the severed head of Medusa, the marriage would be off.

Artistic Depictions of Medusa

Medusa is arguably the best-known monster in all of Greek mythology. That certainly explains why she and her repulsive sisters—together called the Gorgons—were frequent subjects of ancient Greek artists. In fact, the ancient Greeks had a specific word for any artistic depiction of a Gorgon—*gorgoneion*. Of the surviving examples, one of the best preserved is a sculpture of Medusa in the ruins of the Temple of Artemis on the island of Corcyra (near Greece's western coast). The work portrays the famous female monster with a chubby body and a face with over-sized eyes and a wide, gaping mouth. The image also depicts her wearing a belt made of hissing snakes. Other typical physical traits of the Gorgons in ancient Greek art include snub noses, beards, protruding teeth or tusks, very long tongues, wings, and claws like those of eagles and other birds of prey. One motivation for Greek artists to so often depict Medusa came from a common folk belief or superstition of the time. It held that a *gorgoneion* could scare away ghosts, curses, and other evil forces.

Zeus, who cared about both Perseus and Danae, realized that his son would not be able to kill Medusa without help. So the next day Perseus received a surprise visit from the messenger god Hermes and war goddess Athena. Hermes told the young man that the Gorgons dwelled on a remote island and gave him the location. The divine messenger also gave Perseus some winged sandals that allowed him to fly and a magical hat that made its wearer invisible. As for Athena, she handed Perseus a highly polished metal shield. When he needed to look at Medusa, she instructed, he should only do so by looking at the Gorgon's reflection in the shield because her reflection was harmless.

Thrilled to receive these useful tools from the two deities, Perseus wasted no time in flying to the Gorgons' island. There, from high above, he viewed something truly disturbing. "No matter where he turned," the first-century-BCE Roman myth teller Ovid wrote, "he saw both man and beast turned into stone, all creatures who had seen Medusa's face."[32]

Perseus killed Medusa, cut off her head, and put it in a sack.

Mere minutes later, while looking at images reflected in his shield, Perseus glimpsed his prey—the hideous Medusa—below. She appeared to be napping atop a large, flat rock. Seeing his chance, the young warrior took a deep breath to steady his nerves and swiftly dove downward. At the last second, the Gorgon abruptly awoke. She seemed to sense that something was amiss, but it was too late for her. Perseus's razor-sharp blade detached her head, which fell into a sack he had brought for that very purpose.

A Name That Evildoers Came to Fear

As he flew away from the Gorgons' island, Perseus at first intended to return to Seriphos and present Medusa's head to Polydectes. But as he passed by the coast of Phoenicia (now Israel), he caught sight of a large crowd of people below. They were watching a young woman being tied to a post near the beach.

Hoping to find out what was happening, the young hero swooped downward and made his way to the local palace, where he met with the king of that land. Named Cepheus, the ruler explained that his high priests had commanded that his daughter, Andromeda, be sacrificed to a horrible sea monster. However, Cepheus added, a local law said that if someone managed to kill the creature, she would be freed.

ANDROMEDA
A Phoenician princess whom the hero Perseus saved from the jaws of a huge sea monster

Hearing that, Perseus leaped back into the air and hurried to the seashore, arriving just as the scaly, multi-legged monster was crawling out of the water. Carefully reaching into his sack, Perseus pulled out Medusa's serpent-haired head and displayed it to the creature, which suddenly stopped. With an agonizing groan, it shook violently for several seconds. Then it suddenly became motionless as its body rapidly congealed into an enormous stone block.

Having been saved at the last moment, Andromeda heartily thanked Perseus. Neither of them expected to fall in love at first sight, but both did just that. And when he told her he needed to finish his journey back to Seriphos, she gladly accompanied him.

Upon reaching the island, Perseus was upset to find that Polydectes was about to wed Danae against her will. Moreover, at that moment the king was gleefully celebrating the upcoming wedding with his nobles in the palace banquet hall. Realizing what he must do, Edith Hamilton wrote, the young hero "went straight to the palace and entered the hall. As he stood at the entrance . . . he drew the eyes of every man there. Then, before they could look away, he held up the Gorgon's head. And at that sight one and all—the cruel king and his servile courtiers—were turned into stone. There they sat, a row of statues."[33]

In this way, Perseus followed up the defeat of two terrifying monsters with the overthrow of a despicable tyrant. Word of these deeds of valor quickly spread. And in the years that followed, his name struck fear into the hearts of evildoers everywhere.

CHAPTER FIVE

Eternal Tales of Love and Lovers

Not all the ancient Greek myths are set in Greece. A few of those stories take place in foreign lands, and one of the best known is the tragic tale of a boy named Pyramus and a girl named Thisbe. They lived in the renowned ancient Middle Eastern city of Babylon (in what is now Iraq). It was inevitable that they would get to know each other because they were close neighbors. In fact, their families' houses shared a common wall. From an early age the two played together, although they were careful not to let their parents see. This was because the adults of the two families did not get along, never interacted, and forbade their children from socializing with each other.

Thus, when Pyramus and Thisbe reached their late teens and fell deeply in love, their parents knew nothing of the relationship. Neither did the adults know that the young lovers had found a small crack in the wall between their houses. Each and every day the two whispered words of love through that tiny opening and told each other how much they longed to become husband and wife.

Eventually, the lovers felt they could no longer bear to live separately and decided to run away together to another city, or even another country if necessary. Pyramus's plan, to which Thisbe agreed, was to meet the following night at a big mulberry tree near one of the city's gates. The tree would be easy to spot in the moonlight, Pyramus said, because it was presently covered with hundreds of snow-white berries. The plan was to quietly slip through the nearby gate when the guard dozed off, as he often did.

PYRAMUS
In a famous ancient love story, a young man who falls in love with a young woman named Thisbe

As it turned out, Thisbe made it to the mulberry tree first. No sooner had she arrived when she caught sight of a young lion near the city's outer wall. The creature's jaws were dripping with blood, evidently from a recent kill, and afraid the big cat might see her as its next meal, the girl ran away. In her haste, however, she dropped her coat. Curious, the lion walked to the garment and sniffed it, dripping some blood on it before losing interest and walking away.

A few minutes later, Pyramus reached the tree. When he saw the footprints of the animal and the bloodstained coat, he assumed that Thisbe must be dead. The young man blamed himself, wrote Michael Grant, "for making her come to such a dangerous place." So, he decided, it was only right that "he too

Pyramus and Thisbe under the mulberry tree, where Thisbe stabbed herself after finding her dead lover.

would die, [and] he plunged his sword into his side and the blood spouted out over the mulberry tree, dyeing its berries dark red." Mere seconds later, Thisbe returned to the tree and saw her dead lover. Overcome with grief, she used his blood-covered sword to stab herself and fell, lifeless, beside him. Ever since, Grant wrote, as if nature or the gods sought to honor the fallen lovers, "the mulberry fruit, when ripe, is always dark red."[34]

The Strongest Force in the Universe?

Whether set in foreign places like Babylon or in cities and towns in the ancient Greek-speaking lands, the Greek myths abound with tales of love and lovers. Moreover, even when love itself is not the central theme, many of the old Greek tales mention in passing people falling in love, often at first sight. In classical Greek society, most marriages were arranged by parents or other family elders. And it was not unusual for young couples to find themselves in loveless marriages. Yet it was understood that romantic, passionate love did exist for those who were lucky enough to find and experience it.

Moreover, the Greeks were almost unique among ancient peoples for viewing the emotion of full-bodied, fervent love as the strongest force in the universe. It was no accident that the main Greek creation story featured Eros—not merely the god of love but the central, guiding force of love itself—bringing order from chaos and light from darkness. Furthermore, in Greek eyes the influence of the power and allure of love were not confined to the creation era. This can be seen in the way Hesiod described Eros as an intrinsic force still guiding and at times manipulating humans in his own time (the 600s BCE). "Love," he wrote, is the "most beautiful of all the deathless gods. He makes men weak. He overpowers the clever mind and tames the spirit in the breasts of men and gods."[35]

The Greeks similarly applied that idea—that love is a fundamental force driving human passions—to Eros's female counterpart. Some myths portrayed Aphrodite, goddess of love, as

Echo's Love for Narcissus

Eurydice was not the only nymph in Greek mythology to fall deeply in love with a handsome human man. Another was Echo, whose tendency to be too talkative got her in trouble with Hera. Hera punished Echo by taking away her ability to speak normally. Thereafter, all the little nymph could do was repeat the last syllables of words people said to her. The Greeks believed that this was the origin of the natural phenomenon called an echo. But although Echo could no longer talk normally, she still frequently fell in love with men, including some who were not worthy of her. That was certainly the case with Narcissus. An incredibly arrogant individual, he totally ignored poor Echo and spent all his time staring at his reflection in the surface of a pond. Meanwhile, quite sadly, Echo reacted to his rejection of her by becoming depressed and stopping eating. As time went on, she grew thinner and thinner until nothing was left of her but her voice, a faint echo of the unfortunate Echo.

vain and rather shallow. But simultaneously, Greek philosopher-scientists described her as possessing potent powers to shape people's lives by making them fall in love. The first-century-BCE Roman thinker Lucretius, who was steeped in Greek philosophy, addressed her, saying, "You alone are the guiding power of the universe, and without you, nothing emerges into the shining sunlit world to grow in joy and loveliness."[36]

The Ill-Fated Loss of Love

Considering these strong beliefs about the powers that Eros and Aphrodite wielded over human emotions, it is hardly surprising that ancient Greek folklore contains numerous stories about romantic love. Some of these tales have happy endings and others do not. In some, for instance, the true depth of the lovers' feelings for each other are revealed only through the death of one or both of them. The sad story of Pyramus and Thisbe is a famous example.

A different, but no less gloomy, example of the ill-fated loss of love is the myth of Orpheus and Eurydice. Orpheus was a talented poet who also composed amazingly beautiful love songs and skillfully played them on his lyre (a small, handheld harp). All who

EURYDICE

A tree nymph who falls deeply in love with the warrior-musician Orpheus

heard his music—people, animals, and even trees, rocks, and other natural objects—were deeply moved by it.

The young man's travels often took him through vast, picturesque forests. And he sometimes stopped to serenade the local animals and trees, along with any nymphs (minor nature goddesses) who happened to dwell there. It was during one of those informal woodland performances that Orpheus met a tree nymph named Eurydice. The two fell instantly and deeply in love, married, and lived happily for several years.

Orpheus could not resist looking back at Eurydice as he was leading her out of the underworld, and she fell back into its depths.

Psyche's First Sight of Eros

In his version of the tale of Psyche and Eros—in a subplot of his novel *The Golden Ass*—the second-century-CE Roman writer Apuleius described the young woman's first sight of her husband's magnificent physical form, saying:

> [As] she gazed repeatedly on the beauty of that divine countenance [physical appearance], she beheld on his golden head his luxuriant hair steeped in ambrosia [fragrant smells]; his neatly pinned ringlets strayed over his milk-white neck and rosy cheeks, some dangling in front and some behind, and their surpassing sheen made even the lamplight flicker. On the winged god's shoulders his dewy wings gleamed white with flashing brilliance; though they lay motionless, the soft and fragile feathers at their tips fluttered in quivering motion. . . . At the foot of the bed lay his bow, quiver, and arrows, the kindly weapons of that great god. . . . Without prompting, Psyche fell in love with Love, being fired more and more with desire for the god of desire. She gazed down on him in distraction and . . . passionately smothered him with wanton kisses.

Apuleius, *The Golden Ass*, trans. P.G. Walsh. Oxford University Press, 1995, pp. 92–93.

The series of events that upended the lovers' lives began when Eurydice was suddenly bitten by a poisonous snake and died a few hours later. Although some nymphs lived a long time, they were not immortal, like the Olympian gods. Soon afterward, as he did with others who passed away, Thanatos, god of death, arrived and led her soul into the dark depths of the underworld.

Distraught by the loss of the love of his life, Orpheus refused to accept the reality of what had happened. He was determined to find a way to get his beloved wife back. In his mind, there was only one way to do that; namely, to travel into the subterranean land of the dead. There, he planned to confront Hades, the god who oversaw that bleak realm.

After many hours of trekking downward into the earth, Orpheus managed to obtain an audience with Hades and boldly demanded he free Eurydice. The god asked why she should be treated any differently than the other residents of his domain. And

Orpheus's answer was to sing a song so beautiful that it made that normally stern, unemotional deity shed tears. As W.H.D. Rouse told it, when the music ended, Hades exclaimed, "Your music is worth a life. Take her and go. But be very careful never to look back at her till you come to your own door."[37]

With his wife following directly behind him, Orpheus heeded the god's warning during the ensuing hours. Although the gifted musician desperately desired to gaze upon her once more, he managed to stifle that powerful urge. However, mere seconds before reaching the earth's sunlit surface, he could no longer fight the temptation. "The lover looked behind him," Ovid wrote, "and straightaway Eurydice slipped back into the depths. Orpheus stretched out his arms, straining to clasp her, but the hapless man touched nothing but yielding air." Calling out a final farewell, "she fell back again into the same place from which she had come."[38]

In Love with the Love God

The touching tale of Orpheus's lost love often brought listeners to tears. To brighten the mood, storytellers typically followed a deeply sad love story with a happier one. One of the latter is the myth of a young princess named Psyche.

The location of the unnamed realm where Psyche's father ruled as king varied according to where her famous story was told. Originally a Greek tale, over time it spread across the Mediterranean world. And the principal surviving version appears as a subplot in the Roman writer Apuleius's novel *The Golden Ass*. Apuleius made Psyche a princess of a mythical kingdom in northern Italy.

PSYCHE
A young princess who falls in love with and marries Eros, god of love

Psyche became renowned throughout the entire world for her incomparable beauty, Apuleius wrote. In fact, she was so physically striking that many people who met her felt she was even more attractive than the love goddess Aphrodite (whom Apuleius called by her Roman name, Venus). As might be expected, this did not sit well

At night, Psyche sneaked into the room where Eros was sleeping and used a lamp so that she could finally see him.

with the goddess, who, in Apuleius's words, complained, "Here am I, the ancient mother of the universe, [forced] to share the glory of my majesty with a mortal maiden!"[39] Determined to punish Psyche for being so beautiful and popular, Aphrodite turned to the god of love, Eros (whom Apuleius called by his Roman name, Cupid). The plan was for him to cause the young woman to fall in love with the ugliest, meanest man in the world, which was sure to make her miserable in the long run.

That scheme did not work, however, in large part because when Eros first laid eyes on Psyche, he instantly fell deeply in love with her. He whisked her away to an isolated, splendidly decorated house. There, he made sure she was comfortable, although he did not reveal himself to her right away. For months, she only heard his voice, and through hearing it she came to love him as much as he loved her. Soon they wed, although for reasons he never explained he continued to remain invisible to her.

Eventually, however, Psyche could take no more of the mystery surrounding her husband. So one night she sneaked into a dark room where he was sleeping and, using an oil lamp, was finally able to see him in the flesh. As Apuleius wrote, she saw "a handsome god lying in a handsome posture. Even the lamplight was cheered and brightened on seeing him." Psyche herself was "awestruck at this wonderful vision."[40]

Meanwhile, on finding out that Eros had married rather than punished the girl, Aphrodite fumed with anger. The goddess sought to find other ways to harm Psyche, but these came to nothing. Wisely, Eros went to Zeus for help. On hearing Psyche's story, Zeus transformed her into a deity and blessed the strong feelings of love she and Eros shared. In time even Aphrodite did the same, realizing that true love should never be discouraged. Rather, as the most precious commodity in the universe, it should be nurtured, and above all cherished always.

SOURCE NOTES

Introduction: How the Greek Myths Came to Be

1. Euripides, *Heracles*, in *Euripides: Medea and Other Plays*, trans. Philip Vellacott. Penguin, 1984, pp. 164, 166.
2. John Camp and Elizabeth Fisher, *The World of the Ancient Greeks*. Thames and Hudson, 2002, pp. 60–61.
3. Thomas R. Martin, *Ancient Greece, from Prehistoric to Hellenistic Times*. Yale University Press, 1996, pp. 36–37.
4. C.M. Bowra, *The Greek Experience*. Barnes and Noble, 1996, p. 32.

Chapter One: Creation of the World, Gods, and Humans

5. Edith Hamilton, *Mythology*. Grand Central, 1999, p. 63.
6. Hamilton, *Mythology*, p. 64.
7. Hesiod, *Theogony*, in *Hesiod and Theognis*, trans. Dorothea Wender. Penguin, 1982, p. 28.
8. Rex Warner, *The Greek Philosophers*. New American Library, 1958, pp. 9–10.
9. Hesiod, *Theogony*, in *Hesiod, the Homeric Hymns, and Homerica*, trans. H.G. Evelyn-White. Harvard University Press, 1982, pp. 129–31.
10. Hesiod, *Theogony*, p. 53.
11. W.H.D. Rouse, *Gods, Heroes and Men of Ancient Greece*. New American Library, 2001, p. 13.
12. Hamilton, *Mythology*, p. 73.

Chapter Two: Clash of Champions: The Trojan War

13. Michael Grant, *The Rise of the Greeks*. Macmillan, 1987, p. 147.
14. Homer, *Iliad*, trans. E.V. Rieu. Penguin, 1989, p. 256.
15. Homer, *Iliad*, p. 314.
16. Quoted in Homer, *Iliad*, p. 314.
17. Homer, *Iliad*, p. 405–6.
18. Hamilton, *Mythology*, p. 196.

Chapter Three: Perilous Voyages of Epic Adventure

19. Homer, *Odyssey*, trans. E.V. Rieu. Penguin, 1987, pp. 142–3.
20. Quoted in Homer, *Odyssey*, p. 142.

21. Quoted in Homer, *Odyssey*, p. 147.
22. Homer, *Odyssey*, p. 348.
23. Joseph Campbell, *The Hero with a Thousand Faces*. Pantheon, 1949, p. 211.
24. Apollonius of Rhodes, *Argonautica*, published as *The Voyage of the Argo*, trans. E.V. Rieu. Penguin, 1971, p. 88.
25. Apollonius of Rhodes, *Argonautica*, p. 89.

Chapter Four: Daring Heroes Who Slew Monsters

26. Plutarch, *Life of Theseus*, in *The Rise and Fall of Athens: Nine Greek Lives by Plutarch*, trans. Ian Scott-Kilvert. Penguin, 1984, p. 24.
27. Plutarch, *Life of Theseus*, p. 27.
28. John Mancini, "The Top Five Dragon-Slayers from Greek Mythology," Classical Wisdom. http://classicalwisdom.com.
29. Rouse, *Gods, Heroes and Men of Ancient Greece*, p. 55.
30. Hamilton, *Mythology*, p. 160.
31. Michael Grant and John Hazel, *Who's Who in Classical Mythology*. Routledge, 2004, p. 165.
32. Ovid, *Metamorphoses*, trans. Rolfe Humphries. University of Indiana Press, 1967, p. 134.
33. Hamilton, *Mythology*, p. 148.

Chapter Five: Eternal Tales of Love and Lovers

34. Michael Grant, *Myths of the Greeks and Romans*. New American Library, 1962, p. 332.
35. Hesiod, *Theogony*, p. 27.
36. Lucretius, *The Nature of the Universe*, trans. R.E. Latham. Penguin, 1962, p. 27.
37. Quoted in Rouse, *Gods, Heroes and Men of Ancient Greece*, p. 144.
38. Ovid, *Metamorphoses*, trans. Mary M. Innes. Penguin, 2006, p. 226.
39. Apuleius, *The Golden Ass*, trans. P.G. Walsh. Oxford University Press, 1995, p. 76.
40. Apuleius, *The Golden Ass*, p. 92.

FOR FURTHER RESEARCH

Books

Kenny Curtis and Jillian Hughes, *Greeking Out: Epic Retellings of Classic Greek Myths*. National Geographic, 2023.

Bernard Evslin, *Bernard Evslin's Greek Mythology*. Graymalkin, 2023.

Robert Graves, *The Golden Fleece*. OverDrive, 2024.

Homer, *The Iliad and the Odyssey*, trans. Samuel Butler. Kathartika, 2021.

Andrew Lang, *Helen of Troy*. OverDrive, 2024.

Xander Liosis, *Greek Mythology: A Stunning Journey Through Ages and Timeless Stories*. Inkwell House, 2023.

Ena Martinez, *Olympian Odyssey: Exploring Greek Gods and Heroes*. Published by the author, 2025.

Internet Sources

American Museum of National History, "Greek Myths." www.amnh.org.

Mark Cartwright, "Greek Mythology," *World History Encyclopedia*, July 29, 2012. www.worldhistory.org.

Mark Cartwright, "Zeus," *World History Encyclopedia*, May 25, 2013. www.worldhistory.org.

Celeste, "10 Stories from Greek Mythology That Kids Will Love," *Family Experiences Blog*, January 6, 2021. https://familyexperiencesblog.com.

Ducksters, "Monsters and Creatures of Greek Mythology," 2025. www.ducksters.com.

Alexander Gale, "5 Love Stories from Greek Mythology," Greek Reporter, February 14, 2023. https://greekreporter.com.

Greeka, "Jason and the Argonauts," 2025. www.greeka.com.

Charlotte Higgins, "Fruits of the Loom: Why Greek Myths Are Relevant for All Time," *The Guardian* (US edition), September 3, 2021. www.theguardian.com.

History.com Editors, "Greek Mythology," History.com, March 2, 2025. www.history.com.

Organizations and Websites

Ancient Greece for Kids
https://greece.mrdonn.org/myths.html
This website features links to thirty-three myths of ancient Greece and other information about the ancient Greeks.

Encyclopedia of Greek Mythology
www.mythweb.com/encyc
This website provides a lot of useful information about both major and minor Greek mythological characters.

Greek Mythology
www.greekmythology.com
Very useful and easy to navigate, this site features a main page containing numerous links to mini-articles about the gods, heroes, and most famous stories of Greek mythology.

Greek Mythology Link
www.maicar.com/GML
This well-thought-out site has a biographical dictionary with more than six thousand entries and some forty-five hundred photos, drawings, and other images.

Hellenic Times
www.thehellenictimes.com
This well-organized, useful site contains several links that lead to substantial articles about diverse aspects of the Greek myths, including their sources, the Greek gods, beasts and monsters, and love stories.

Theoi Greek Mythology
www.theoi.com
This is unarguably the most comprehensive and reliable general website about Greek mythology on the internet. It features hundreds of separate pages filled with detailed, accurate information, as well as numerous primary sources and reproductions of ancient paintings and mosaics.

INDEX

Note: Boldface page numbers indicate illustrations.

PICTURE CREDITS

Cover: ZU_09/Shutterstock

4: Shutterstock.com
7: Science History Images/Alamy Stock Photo
12: CBW/Alamy Stock Photo
15: Dipper Historic/Alamy Stock Photo
18: Ivy Close Images/Universal Images Group/Newscom
22: Chronicle/Alamy Stock Photo
25: Luisa Ricciarini/Bridgeman Images
27: Chronicle/Alamy Stock Photo
32: Ivy Close Images/Alamy Stock Photo
34: Chronicle/Alamy Stock Photo
37: Chronicle/Alamy Stock Photo
40: Ivy Close Images/Alamy Stock Photo
44: Heritage Image Partnership Ltd/Alamy Stock Photo
46: Adam Eastland/Alamy Stock Photo
50: World History Archive/Alamy Stock Photo
53: Charles Walker Collection/Alamy Stock Photo
56: Peter Horree/Alamy Stock Photo

ABOUT THE AUTHOR

Classical historian and award-winning author Don Nardo has written numerous acclaimed volumes about ancient civilizations and peoples. They include more than four dozen overviews of the mythologies of the Sumerians, Babylonians, Egyptians, Greeks, Romans, Persians, Celts, Aztecs, Norse, Chinese, Japanese, and others. Nardo, who also composes and arranges orchestral music, lives with his wife Christine in Massachusetts.